DENTAL ASSISTING

A Career That Makes You Smile
and Earns You Money

DENTAL ASSISTING

A Career That Makes You Smile
and Earns You Money

DR. KIMBERLY HARPER, DDS

purposely
created
PUBLISHING

DENTAL ASSISTING
Published by Purposely Created Publishing Group™
Copyright © 2018 Kimberly Harper
All rights reserved.

Printed in the United States of America
ISBN: 978-1-948400-66-4

Special discounts are available on bulk quantity purchases by book clubs, associations and special interest groups. For details email: sales@publishyourgift.com or call (888) 949-6228.
For information logon to: www.PublishYourGift.com

To the amazing dental assistants I have had the privilege of working with over the past fourteen years of my dental career: thank you for all you have taught me about the wonderful career of dental assisting. To all future dental assistants: I wrote this book to help you explore the many opportunities available to you in this amazing, fun career. I wish you the best of luck!

TABLE OF CONTENTS

Dr. Kimberly Harper, DDS

INTRODUCTION

Welcome to the wonderful career of dental assisting. In this book, I'm going to share with you information and knowledge that will assist you in your career, no matter where you are on this journey. This book is for you if you are considering a career in dental assisting, if you are in school to become a dental assistant, or if you are already working as a dental assistant. So, listen up.

What is a dental assistant? A dental assistant is a skilled individual who assists the dentist. Training and skills are taught through various programs, which you will learn about in this book. Their duties cover a vast array of topics and procedures. There are positions working with general dentists as well as with specialists. You can even advance to other areas of dentistry with additional training and experience.

Still not sure about a career in dental assisting? Let me share with you a well-known secret in the dental world: dental assistants are the life of the dental office. You will be the dentist's right hand. We cannot work without you. You make our jobs so much easier, and we appreciate you for that. You are a valuable component of the dental office.

Who am I and why did I write this book?

As a dentist in private practice for fourteen years, I have worked with some amazing dental assistants. I have learned a lot about the career and have noticed that it is sometimes overlooked as a career choice. Making a decision about your future is tough. It can feel overwhelming at times. There are so many choices and so many opinions from others. I totally get it. I was there too. That is why I decided to write a book about the wonderful career of dental assisting. I want to shed some light on this great opportunity that most people don't think about when choosing a career. I want to give you the inside scoop and let you know how easy it is to become a dental assistant, get a job, and start making money.

In this book, I'm going to walk you through the three stages of becoming a dental assistant and answer some of the most common questions I hear at each stage of this process.

Stage 1 of becoming a dental assistant is Before School. During this phase, you may be questioning if dental assisting is for you. Question no more; I have included a short quiz to help you determine if you have the right traits to become an excellent dental assistant. I will also cover what is required of a dental assistant, the duties and responsibilities of a dental assistant, and how you become a dental assistant. If you are interested in teeth but are not sure if dental assisting is for you, Stage 1 will give you great insight into what your life will be like as a dental assistant.

Stage 2 of becoming a dental assistant is During School. You made the decision to become a dental assistant. Now what? You may be thinking about which school to apply to or what you will learn. In this stage of the book, I will share with you what you will learn in the dental assisting program, dental terms and knowledge, and pros and cons of the different programs that are available to you. I will also cover different employment opportunities you can consider after graduation.

The final stage of this process is Stage 3, After School. This section covers some of the important questions you may have. Questions like: how much money will I make? Will I get a job? What else can I do in the dental field? In this section, I will share with you the number one quality most dental offices are looking for when hiring a dental assistant. I will give you interview tips and sample interview questions with suggested answers. I will also share with you the secret to earning more money as a dental assistant.

So, what are you waiting for? Let's get started!

BEFORE SCHOOL

CHAPTER 1

HOW DO YOU KNOW DENTAL ASSISTING IS FOR YOU?

So, you may be asking whether dental assisting is for you. No worries. The following quiz will help you discover if you have the qualities to become an excellent dental assistant. I believe you do. Let's take the quiz.

1. Do you like helping others?	YES	NO
2. Do you enjoy working as a team?	YES	NO
3. Are you organized?	YES	NO
4. Do you pay close attention to detail?	YES	NO
5. Are you a good listener?	YES	NO
6. Are you passionate about oral hygiene and dental health?	YES	NO
7. Do you put people at ease?	YES	NO
8. Are you personable?	YES	NO
9. Are you a good communicator?	YES	NO
10. Do you enjoy working with your hands?	YES	NO
11. Do you communicate effectively?	YES	NO
12. Are you comfortable with bodily fluids like blood and saliva?	YES	NO

Let's total your points. Each "YES" answer is 1 point, and each "NO" answer is 0 points. Check the score card below.

7 to 12 points—Congratulations! You are a future dental assistant. You possess many traits that ensure success in dental assisting.

2 to 6 points—You possess some of the traits needed to succeed in the career of dental assisting. With a little hard work, you can be an excellent dental assistant.

0 to 2 points—As a dental assistant, you can work in many different positions within the dental office, all requiring a different set of skills. Don't give up. We're going to find a perfect fit for you.

CHAPTER 2

WHAT IS REQUIRED OF A DENTAL ASSISTANT?

Dental assistants have a very important role in the dental office. They must connect and build relationships with the patients, the dentist, and other team members. Here are five traits you must have to succeed in a career as a dental assistant:

1. Great Personality

2. Great People Skills

3. Well Organized

4. Attention to Detail

5. Professionalism

Great Personality: Dental assistants are the social butterflies of the dental practice. The number one priority of a dental assistant is to build a relationship with the patient and to make them comfortable while in the dental chair. Most patients are nervous about going to the dentist. Having a great personality will allow you to excel at making your patients feel comfortable and at ease while receiving dental treatment. This will make the dentist happy as well as the patient. Your great personality will be an asset to your other team members, too. Getting along with your team members is very important and can make it a great day in the office for the whole team.

Great People Skills: Building a relationship with patients requires great people skills. Knowing how to talk to your patients is invaluable, as you must choose the right words, select the correct tone, and, most of all, listen to your patients. As you will learn in a few chapters, there are a lot of dental terms used to describe your teeth and the condition of your mouth. Once you learn these terms during your training program, they will become second nature to you. But you must remember to keep it simple. No one likes to be talked down to, especially your patients. Speak "dental jargon" with your team members, but remember to speak in simple terms when discussing dentistry with your patient.

Selecting the right tone can mean the difference between being informative and condescending. We have all said something to someone and not realized it was offensive until it was pointed out. We have all experienced a loved one saying something to us in a harsh tone that maybe hurt our feelings. We know they did not mean it, but it still hurt. So, be mindful of how you speak to your patients. Speak to them in a respectful and caring manner.

The number one secret to building relationships with patients is listening. Most patients want to be heard and to express their concerns. As they get to know you more, they will want to share their life stories with you. As a dental assistant, you should want to learn more about them and accept that invitation into their world. Ask about their children, their pets, their job, or their grandkids. Share your stories with them, but, most of all, listen.

Well Organized: As a dental assistant you will have many responsibilities and duties. There are important tasks to complete and stay on top of during the work day. You are a key part of the dental team and several team members are depending on you, as well as the patients. Keeping all the supplies organized for the team, keeping the tray organized for the dentist, and keeping track of the schedule are just a few of your many duties. Being organized will help you and your team flow through the day better and go home feeling rewarded and accomplished. We will review the responsibilities and duties of a dental assistant in a later chapter.

Attention to Detail: Safety is a key component of your career as a dental assistant. Radiation safety, infection control, and HIPPA and OSHA regulations are all part of keeping the patient safe. Good attention to detail will help you adhere to the many government and federal health regulations. This will help the patient, protect the dentist and the other team members, and allow the office to operate safely.

Professionalism: Your appearance and how you carry yourself says a lot about who you are as a person. When you feel good about yourself, you treat others well. By dressing appropriately and possessing a good attitude, you are providing a great service to your patients and your team. Don't forget to SMILE!

CHAPTER 3

WHAT ARE THE DUTIES AND RESPONSIBILITIES OF A DENTAL ASSISTANT?

A dental assistant is a critical player in helping the dentist take care of the patient's oral health. In most cases, the dental assistant becomes the dentist's right hand, like an extension of the dentist. They become partners in caring for the patients. The dentist cannot work without the dental assistant and vice versa. Dental assistants perform a wide range of duties within the dental office. These duties can include preparing the treatment room for the patient, sterilizing equipment and instruments, updating the patient chart, and ordering supplies. Dental assistants also have the responsibility of supporting the dentist during procedures, maintaining a sterile work environment, and educating the patient about their dental care. Feeling overwhelmed? Don't worry. All the duties and responsibilities of a dental assistant will become routine in no time.

A DAY IN THE LIFE OF A DENTAL ASSISTANT

Here are some of the typical daily duties you can expect to perform when you become a dental assistant:

- Meet and greet your patients.

- Help the patient feel comfortable before, during, and after treatment.

- Review the patient's health history, noting any changes.

- Take the patient's blood pressure and document it in their chart.

- Take dental x-rays and photos. Set up and break down the patient treatment room.

- Assist the dentist during a variety of treatment procedures.

- Pass instruments and materials to the dentist.

- Suction the patient's mouth while the dentist works.

- Serve as an infection control officer.

- Develop and implement infection control protocols.

- Sterilize and disinfect dental instruments and equipment.

- Prepare tray setups for dental procedures.

- Take impressions of the patient's teeth for study casts.

- Apply topical anesthetic prior to injection.

- Provide post-operative instructions prescribed by the dentist.

- Instruct patients in oral hygiene techniques to maintain oral health.

- Explain dental procedures.

- Make temporary crowns.

- Pour up impressions of the patient's mouth.

- Make mouth guards and bleaching trays.

- Clean and polish removable appliances.

- Order supplies and materials.

- Maintain an inventory of supplies.

You may be asked to assist the front office team as well. Here are a few front office duties you can expect to perform when you become a dental assistant:

- Schedule and confirm appointments.

- Verify dental insurance.

- Check patients in and out.

- Answer the office phone.

- Review recommended treatment with patients.

- Make payment arrangements.

Each office has its own requirements and expectations of a dental assistant. Completing a dental assisting program will give you the basic knowledge to enter the career of dental assisting, but you will learn and do different things in different offices over the course of your career.

CHAPTER 4

HOW DO YOU BECOME
A DENTAL ASSISTANT?

Good news! You can become a dental assistant in just twelve weeks with only a high school education. No college degree is required. Some training programs are more affordable than a four-year college degree. You can spend less time in school, find a job quicker, and start making money right after you graduate from the program.

So, what are these programs, you ask?

When applying to dental assisting programs, you have a few options: career or trade schools, in-office schools, or community colleges or universities. Let's explore your options for becoming a dental assistant.

OPTION 1: CAREER OR TRADE SCHOOL

A career or trade school is a post-secondary education designed to teach technical skills required for a specific job.

PROS

- Cheaper than a four-year college degree, but still quite expensive
  - » $12,000–15,000
- Shorter than a four-year college degree
- Certification

CONS

- Expensive
- Nine- to twelve-month program
- Minimal hands-on experience

OPTION 2: IN-OFFICE SCHOOLS

In-office schools are twelve-week educational programs taught in a dental office.

PROS

- Short term—twelve weeks
- Costs less than either a career school or a community college or university
- Hands-on experience
- Certification

CONS

- Fast-paced
- No financial aid

OPTION 3: COMMUNITY COLLEGE OR UNIVERSITY

A community college typically offers two years of college courses and an associate's degree upon completion. Credits earned at a community college can be used to transfer to a four-year university to graduate with a bachelor's degree.

PROS

- Graduating with an associate's or bachelor's degree
- Better career opportunities
- Higher income

CONS

- Spending two to four years in school
- Student loans
- Difficult time finding a job after graduation

Now that you know how to become a dental assistant, what are you waiting for? Let's apply.

DURING SCHOOL

CHAPTER 5

WHAT AM I GOING TO LEARN IN DENTAL ASSISTING SCHOOL?

Congratulations! You have been accepted into dental assisting school. You may be wondering, "What am I going to learn?" Of course, every program is different, but in general, you will learn about teeth and gums, oral diseases, and dental procedures.

As an example, here is a list of courses from The Dental Assisting Academy curriculum:

- Dental Module 1: Introduction to Dentistry and Dental Assisting

  This subject introduces students to the field of dentistry and dental assisting, plus dental terminology and tooth anatomy.

- Dental Module 2: Infection Prevention and Hazardous Materials

  This subject introduces students to infection control. Students will learn how to prevent disease transmission with infection control as well as instrument management.

- <u>Dental Module 3: Patient Management</u>

  This subject introduces students to patient management. Students will learn how to properly manage the patient, from establishing the dental record to protocols for medical emergencies in the dental office. Tools will be given to effectively manage dental anxiety and pain.

- <u>Dental Module 4: Dental Imaging</u>

  This subject introduces students to dental imaging. Upon completion of this subject, students will understand radiation safety, production, and protocols for oral radiography.

- <u>Dental Module 5: Clinical Dentistry</u>

  This subject introduces students to clinical dentistry. Upon completion of this subject, students will understand the dental office layout and functions of the various spaces in the practice of dentistry, tools for proper isolation, and the field of preventive dentistry and common procedures utilized for dental prevention. Students will learn instrument transfer and four-handed dentistry.

- Dental Module 6: Dental Specialties 1

  This subject introduces students to dental specialties—operative and cosmetic dentistry. Upon completion of this subject, the students will understand the purpose and types of procedures utilized in operative dentistry, the dental materials and equipment utilized during restorative procedures, and the primary procedures involved in cosmetic dentistry.

- Dental Module 7: Dental Materials and Lab Procedures

  This subject introduces students to dental materials and lab procedures. Upon completion, the students will understand the tools used for impression making as well as the different types of impressions, the steps involved from the impression to the cast fabrication, and the purpose of various casts used in restorative dentistry.

- Dental Module 8: Dental Specialties 2

  Upon completion of this subject, students will understand and be able to assist for endodontic, oral and maxillofacial surgery, pediatric, orthodontics, and periodontal procedures.

- Dental Module 9: Front Office

  This subject introduces the students to front office administration. Upon completion, the students will understand and be able to answer the phone properly, schedule an appointment, and verify insurance.

- Dental Module 10: Preparation for Employment

  This subject introduces students to resume writing and job interview skills. Upon completion of this subject, students will be prepared for employment.

- Dental Module 11: Preparation for DANB Exam

  This subject reviews all materials and procedures to prepare students for the Dental Assisting National Board Exam (DANB). Upon completion, students will be prepared and ready for the national exam.

- Dental Module 12: Externship

  This subject is a hands-on externship that is completed in an operating dental office with live patients. Students will apply the many lessons learned in lecture and lab. Upon completion, students will be prepared to work as a dental assistant.

Each module is followed up with a separate, practical lab session. During the lab session, the hands-on portion of each module is taught and practiced. Upon completion, you will know how to perform most of the required duties of a dental assistant.

At the end of your dental assisting program, you will receive a certificate of completion. This certificate will allow you to register with your State Board of Dental Examiners once you have completed the Dental Assisting National Board Exam (DANB). This exam will include Radiation Health and Safety (RHS), Infection Control (ICE), and General Chairside (GC). Preparation for this exam is usually included in the dental assisting curriculum. You will be required to renew your certificate yearly for a small renewal fee and complete a certain number of continuing education hours. The number of continuing education hours varies from state to state. Once you complete the exam and register with the state, you are considered a Registered Dental Assistant (RDA) and a Certified Dental Assistant (CDA). These two titles can be used interchangeably, but RDA seems to be most common.

CHAPTER 6

FACTS ABOUT YOUR TEETH AND GUMS

Here are ten fun facts about your teeth and gums:

1. Teeth start to form even before you are born. Baby teeth start to form while the baby is still in the womb and do not come through until the child is between six to twelve months old. Children usually have around twenty teeth by the age of three.

2. As adults, we each have thirty-two teeth in our mouth, including four different types of teeth—incisors, canines, premolars, and molars. We use them to cut, tear, and grind our food.

3. The white outer part of your tooth is called enamel. It is the hardest part of your entire body.

4. We only have two sets of teeth in our life-time—baby teeth and permanent teeth.

5. No two people have the same set of teeth. Your teeth are as unique as your fingerprints.

6. An average person spends 38.5 days brushing their teeth over a lifetime.

7. Many diseases are linked to your oral health, including heart disease, osteoporosis, and diabetes.

8. Your mouth produces over twenty-five thousand quarts of saliva in a lifetime. Saliva aids with digestion of your food and protects your teeth from bacteria in your mouth.

9. Only two-thirds of your tooth length is visible in your mouth. The remaining one-third is underneath your gums.

10. If you get your tooth knocked out, put it in milk and get to a dentist right away. The milk will help your tooth survive longer.

CHAPTER 7

DENTAL JARGON

Now that you have learned some interesting facts about your teeth and gums, let's dive a little deeper and learn some of the basic dental terms you will use every day in your new career as a dental assistant.

- Abscess: an infection of a tooth, soft tissue, or bone.

- Amalgam: a "silver" filling material used for fillings that contains mercury, silver, tin, copper, and sometimes zinc.

- Anesthetic: medication used to eliminate pain. Local anesthetic is used for numbing the tooth, and general anesthetic produces unconsciousness.

- Bicuspid: the next two teeth located after the canine, making eight total. They are used for chewing.

- Bitewing: a type of x-ray used to show the teeth from the crown of the tooth to the level of bone.

- Bonding: a procedure to enhance the appearance of the teeth using composite resin materials.

- Bridge: a fixed appliance used to replace one or more missing teeth. A bridge is cemented or bonded to the supporting teeth.

- Bruxism: Grinding of teeth during sleep.

- Bur: small metal attachment used in the dentist drill for cutting or smoothing a tooth.

- Calculus: hard, calcium-like deposits that form on teeth due to inadequate oral care. Usually appears yellow or brown. Also called "tartar."

- Composite: tooth-colored filling material composed of resin material. An alternative to silver amalgam fillings.

- Crown (or Cap): a dental restoration covering all or most of the natural tooth. A crown can be made of porcelain, composite, or metal. It is cemented into place.

- Cuspid: The third tooth from the center of the mouth. Also called "canines," "fangs," or "eye teeth."

- Plaque: a sticky film that forms on the teeth. Plaque not removed daily eventually turns into tartar and calculus.

- Prophylaxis: cleaning of the teeth to prevent periodontal disease and decay.

- Prosthetic: a fixed or removable appliance used to replace missing teeth.

- Pulp: the living part of the tooth. Also called the "nerve."

- Root: the portion of the tooth that is in the bone.

- Root Canal Therapy: procedure used to save a tooth in which the pulp or nerve is removed and filled with a permanent filling.

- Saliva: clear, lubricating fluid in the mouth.

- Scaling and Root Planning: a deep-cleaning, non-surgical procedure performed to remove plaque and tartar from above and below the gum line.

- Sealant: a thin, clear or white resin material applied to the chewing surface of teeth to prevent decay.

- Supernumerary Tooth: an extra tooth.

- Decay: destruction of tooth structure caused by acid produced by bacteria. Also called "cavities" or "caries."

- Deciduous Teeth: commonly called "baby teeth" or "primary teeth."

- Dentin: inner layer of a tooth.

- Denture: a removable replacement for missing teeth and surrounding tissue.

- Edentulous: having no teeth.

- Enamel: the white outer covering of each tooth.

- Extraction: the removal of a tooth.

- Filling: restoration of lost tooth structure with metal, porcelain, or resin materials.

- Flossing: cleaning between the teeth using a thread-like material.

- Fluoride: a mineral that helps strengthen teeth enamel, making teeth less susceptible to decay.

- Gingiva: the soft tissue that surrounds the base of the teeth. Also called "gums."

- Gingivitis: inflammation of gum tissue that may bleed easily when touched or brushed.

- Halitosis: chronic bad breath.
- Handpiece: the instrument used by the dentist to cut or smooth the tooth.
- Hygienist: a licensed dental professional who uses preventive, therapeutic, and educational methods to control oral disease.
- Impacted tooth: a tooth that is partially or completely blocked from erupting through the gums.
- Implant: a titanium rod that is surgically placed into the jawbone where a tooth is missing. It serves as the tooth root for the crown, bridge, or denture that is placed over it.
- Impression: mold made of the teeth and gums.
- Jawbone: bone which anchors the teeth.
- Mandible: lower jaw.
- Maxilla: upper jaw.
- Molar: three back teeth used for grinding food.
- Night Guard: a removable acrylic appliance that fits over the upper or lower teeth

and is used to prevent wear and damage to the teeth caused by grinding of the teeth during sleeping.

- Nitrous Oxide: a gas used to reduce patient anxiety.
- Occlusion: the relationship of the upper and lower teeth when the mouth is closed.
- Oral hygiene: procedures used to maintain a clean, healthy mouth.
- Panoramic X-ray: a type of x-ray that shows a complete 2-D representation of all the teeth in the mouth. This x-ray also shows the relationship of the teeth to the jaw and the jaw to the rest of the head.
- Palate: hard and soft tissue forming the roof of the mouth.
- Periapical X-rays: x-rays providing complete views of the teeth, from the roots the crowns of the teeth.
- Periodontitis: a more advanced stage gum disease in which the gums and bone pull away from the teeth and form pockets and in which alveolar bone is destroyed.
- Permanent Teeth: adult teeth.

- Tooth Whitening: procedure used to whiten the teeth.

- Veneer: a thin, custom-made shell of tooth-colored porcelain or resin bonded directly to the front side of the natural tooth to improve the appearance.

- Wisdom Teeth: third molars that usually erupt from age eighteen to twenty-five.

- X-ray: high-frequency radiation that penetrates different substances with different rates of absorption.

CHAPTER 8

LOOKING AHEAD . . . WHERE WILL I WORK AS A DENTAL ASSISTANT?

Employment opportunities in the field of dentistry are excellent. There are many types of dental practices to choose from. Here is a list of the most common work environments for dental assistants:

- Solo Dental Practice: This is a general dentistry practice with only one dentist and two to four dental assistants. This type of dental practice is a great opportunity if you work better in small groups and enjoy close relationships and connections. This type of dental practice will feel like family.

- Group Dental Practice: Group practices have two or more dentists and six to ten dental assistants. This type of dental practice is a great learning opportunity, especially for new graduates. It is a general dentistry practice. The skill level of the dental assistants varies from new graduates to those with ten or more years of experience in the dental field. This is a great place to work on your speed, efficiency, and technique. It's also a great place to experience a large variety of procedures.

- Specialty Practice: There are nine dental specialties recognized by the American Dental Association. Working with a specialist may require a little more training, but can be very rewarding if you are interested in a particular specialty. Here is a list of specialty dental practices you can consider:

  » Oral Surgery: Removal of teeth and correction of facial deformities.

  » Endodontist: Root canal treatment.

  » Periodontist: Treatment of gum problems.

  » Orthodontist: Straightening teeth with braces or other appliances.

  » Prosthodontist: Replacement of lost teeth.

  » Pediatrics: Treatment of children.

- » Public Health: Prevention of dental disease through organized community effort.

- » Oral Pathology: Identification and management of oral diseases.

- » Oral Radiology: Interpretation of dental images.

- Hospital Dental Practice: This is a general dentistry or specialty dental practice located in a hospital. In this type of dental practice, you will be assisting the dentist in treating bedridden patients. This type of dental practice is good if you enjoy caring for patients with long-term illnesses and working shift hours.

- Dental School Clinics: In this type of dental practice, you will be assisting dental students as they learn to perform dental procedures. This can be general dentistry or specialty. Dental school clinics are a great opportunity to learn more about the dental profession. They are slower paced and provide a wealth of dental knowledge.

AFTER SCHOOL

CHAPTER 9

APPLYING FOR YOUR
FIRST JOB

Congratulations! You've completed your dental assisting program. Now it's time to apply for your very first job in your new career. Most dental offices will request a copy of your resume. You will probably prepare your resume while in the dental assisting program.

WHERE SHOULD YOU APPLY?

Once your resume is completed, you can apply for jobs online. There are many websites to look at for job postings in the dental field. Here are a few places to get started:

- www.dentalpost.com
- www.dentalworkers.com
- www.craigslist.org
- www.careerbuilder.com
- www.simplyhired.com
- www.ihiredental.com

- www.facebook.com
- www.indeed.com
- www.monster.com

When corresponding with a future employer, remember to have a professional email address. For example, Partygirl275@gmail.com may not be an appropriate email address. Using your first and last name, first initial and last name, or any variation of your name is a good option. You can also add numbers or "RDA" at the end of your name. Rachelgarrisonrda@gmail.com is a great example of a professional email address.

Registering with a temporary agency is a good way to gain experience and explore different offices. Some agencies are willing to accept new graduates and some are not. Simply do an online search for dental temporary agencies in your area and give a few of them a call. Most will ask for a copy of your resume and some will ask you to come in for an interview. There are interview tips in the next chapter.

Another way to look for a job is the old-fashioned "door to door" technique. Dropping off your resume at dental offices near you is a great way to find job opportunities nearby. It allows the dental team to see you and connect with you in person rather than on paper. Be sure to wear professional attire and smile. Don't be afraid to inquire about their current job openings.

WHAT ARE DENTAL OFFICES LOOKING FOR IN A STRONG CANDIDATE?

The number one quality that dental offices are looking for is CONFIDENCE.

As a dental assistant, you will be a key player in building relationships with the patients and making them feel comfortable in the dental chair. To the patient, you are the dental expert. Most patients feel more comfortable asking you questions than asking the dentist. So, believe in yourself and be confident. Dental offices want to know that their patients are being taken care of and they are trusting you to do it.

Here is a list of some additional qualities a strong candidate should possess to be hired as a dental assistant:

- Likes helping others.
- Caring.
- Compassionate.

- A team player, works well with others.
- Able to multi-task.
- Detail-oriented.
- Willingness to learn.
- Dependable.
- Independent thinker.
- Self-motivated.
- Honest.
- Friendly.
- Fast learner.
- Efficient.
- Flexible.

Be sure to list your BEST qualities on your resume. Include good professional references, not your friends or family members. Include any volunteer work you have done, as well as interests and hobbies. You should also list any groups or clubs you may be involved with.

CHAPTER 10

HOW TO MASTER
THE INTERVIEW

You landed your first job interview as a dental assistant. Congrats! The interview is the second step of the hiring process and may be conducted by the office manager, the dentist, or another team member. During the interview, you will be evaluated by the way you present yourself. The person conducting the interview will evaluate your personality and your attitude. So, let your personality shine, make eye contact, and SMILE!

Most people are usually very nervous about the interview, but don't worry. Here are several Dos and Don'ts that will help you master the interview.

- Be early for your interview, not just on time.
- Turn off your cell phone.
- Wear professional attire. Your appearance is very important!
- Make eye contact.
- Smile.

- Do not fidget.
- Do not ramble.
- Keep your answers simple.
- Do not say negative things about a former boss, manager, or coworker.
- Be authentic.
- Practice answering interview questions.

Here are a few standard interview questions you may be asked and the best way to answer them:

1. *Why did you leave your last job?*

   "I wanted to get into the dental field."

   "I've always been interested in teeth."

   "I want to help people."

   "I decided to change careers."

Keep this answer simple and positive. Don't give too much detail and do not say anything negative about your previous job.

2. *What makes you the best candidate for this job?*

   "I'm outgoing, caring, dependable, and always willing to learn. I like getting along with others and I'm a team player."

Remember to always list your best qualities. Use the list from the previous chapter for ideas of what to emphasize.

3. *Tell me a little bit about yourself.*

> "I'm from the Irving area and I attended MacArthur High School. I love animals and I have two dogs and a cat. I decided to become a dental assistant because I enjoy helping others and I have always been interested in teeth."

Get comfortable talking about yourself. Decide on three things you would like to share with the interviewer and use that statement for each interview.

Some offices may ask you to come in for a working interview. A working interview is an opportunity for the dental office to see how you work and if you get along with the current team members. It is also an opportunity to see if the office is a fit for you. This may be for a half day or a full day. Some offices pay you for the working interview. The same interview tips apply, but here are a few more that are specific to the working interview:

- Ask the interviewer what you should wear.

- Take notes. Bring a small notebook and pen.

- Ask questions.

- Do not chew gum.

- Keep busy.

- Ask the team members if there is anything you can help them with.

How you end your interview is very important. At the end of your interview, extend your hand and thank the interviewer for the opportunity. Let them know they have a nice staff and a beautiful office and that it was a pleasure to meet them. You never get a second chance to make a first impression!

Now that you know the number one quality that dental offices are looking for in a dental assistant, top interview tips, and sample interview questions, you should have no problems getting that first job, even without any dental experience.

CHAPTER 11

HOW MUCH MONEY
AM I GOING TO MAKE?

Employment of dental assistants will continue to grow as ongoing research continues to link oral health and systemic health. Dentists will continue to hire dental assistants to help make their job of delivering dental care more efficient. More dental assistants will be needed as dental practices continually grow.

Now that job security has been established, let's talk about salary. The average annual salary of a dental assistant ranges from $25,460 to $52,000, according to the US Bureau of Labor Statistics. The average hourly rate is $18.22. Salary varies between each state and depends on the experience, location, education, or certification of the dental assistant.

Pay raises for a dental assistant are based on job performance, length of employment, and position in the dental office.

Do you want to know the secret to earning more money?

Dr. Kimberly Harper, DDS

BE INVALUABLE TO YOUR DENTIST!

Go the extra mile. Be willing to stay late or come in early. Be helpful. Do all that you can to make his or her day run smoother.

CHAPTER 12

WHAT'S NEXT?

There are many career opportunities available to you once you become a dental assistant. Some dental assistants go on to become dental hygienists or even dentists. Both of those careers require additional years of education. Dental hygiene school requires prerequisites and completion of a two-year program. Dentists typically attend an undergraduate college or university for four years and dental school for an additional four years.

If spending more time in school is not for you, there are many ways you can leverage your dental assisting education. Most dental assistants will help the front office team members from time to time. This can include answering the phone, verifying insurance, scheduling appointments, and reviewing patient treatment plans. These skills can help you advance to an office manager position.

Other career opportunities include working for an insurance company processing dental insurance claims, being a dental product sales representative, or working at a dental laboratory making dentures, crowns, and bridges.

Once you become a dental assistant, the sky is the limit. How far you go is up to you!

Thank You

Thank you for purchasing and reading this book. I hope you learned something new about the career of dental assisting that will help you make a decision about your future. I wish you the best in any career that you choose! If you have more questions about dental assisting or other career choices, connect with me using the various sources below. Best of luck!

Website:

www.thedentalassistingacademy.com

Facebook:

www.facebook.com/thedentalassistingacademy

YouTube:

www.youtube.com/thedentalassistingacademy

Instagram:

www.instagram.com/thedentalassistingacademy

About the Author

Dr. Kimberly Harper is a cosmetic and restorative dentist. She is passionate about helping others, and her professional life is centered around improving people's confidence by enhancing their smiles. One way she helps others is through her yearly mission trips to provide dental care to those in need in other countries.

Dr. Kimberly believes in developing a relationship with each of her patients to better listen to their needs and provide them with the best possible care. Along with her private dental practice, Dr. Kimberly is also the founder and dean of the Dental Assisting Academy, a twelve-week educational program that prepares students for certification as a dental assistant. She also has a YouTube channel, "Dr. Kimberly DDS," where she shares her knowledge of dentistry.

Dr. Kimberly can be contacted through her website, www.thedentalassistingacademy.com

CREATING DISTINCTIVE BOOKS
WITH INTENTIONAL RESULTS

We're a collaborative group of creative masterminds
with a mission to produce high-quality books to position
you for monumental success in the marketplace.

Our professional team of writers, editors, designers,
and marketing strategists work closely together to ensure
that every detail of your book is a clear representation
of the message in your writing.

Want to know more?
Write to us at info@publishyourgift.com
or call (888) 949-6228

Discover great books, exclusive offers, and more at
www.PublishYourGift.com

Connect with us on social media

@publishyourgift

CPSIA information can be obtained
at www.ICGtesting.com
Printed in the USA
LVHW021532041218
599237LV00018B/485/P